Retirement Book Camp:

Your Ultimate Retirement Guide

Copyright © 2014 by Richard Stanton
All rights reserved.

No part of this publication may be reproduced, distributed, or transmitted in any form or by any means, including photocopying, recording, or other electronic or mechanical methods, without the prior written permission of the publisher, except in the case of brief quotations embodied in critical reviews and certain other noncommercial uses permitted by copyright law. For permission requests, write to the publisher.

First Printing, 2014
Fusion Publications, LLC

Copyright © 2014 Fusion Publications

ISBN-13: 978-1505216820

ISBN-10: 1505216826

1 3 5 7 9 10 8 6 4 2

To my parents, for a much deserved and well-earned retirement

Retirement Book Camp: Your Ultimate Retirement Guide

Table of Contents

Table of Contents……………………………………………..8

Foreword ………………………………………………..10

Introduction………………………………………………17

Topic One: The Journey Begins……………………………………………28

Mental Adjustment……………………………………………..31

Physical Adjustment……………………………………………..34

Spiritual Adjustment…………………………………………….38

Topic Two: Managing Money……………………………………………….43

Topic Three: Family Life...63

Topic Four: Dealing with Loss..80

Topic Five: Being Tech Savvy..89

Conclusion...98

Retirement Book Camp Checklist...102

FOREWARD

Welcome to retirement! Welcome to a new brave new transition that we all must eventually deal with – some better than others. Some may believe that people who are 65 plus years of age and are making the most out of retirement may be few in number but in actuality they are all over and not because they are the chosen ones. It is because they have decided once not to live in denial.

Living in denial is something that has destroyed so many people socially, psychologically and mentally. For many people who would love to ensure that everything is going as planned and that they will always be victorious in one way or the other. But since they don't have any plan, persist in maintaining the status quo even when it is clearly not working, or choose to isolate themselves in perpetuity believing, sadly, that they will be better off and content that way.

This book will give you powerful tools and important tips that you can follow to ensure that you are the real deal in terms of creating a unique retirement package targeted not for "everyone"; but individually suited just for you and your specific needs as a unique individual. Let us not make excuses about why we can't have a happy retirement as there really are none. People who come up with tired excuses and reasons why they can't be happy or can't be successful or can't possibly have a meaningful and satisfying relationship with their loved ones and so on don't really believe in themselves in the sense that they just have to come up with something to prolong their misery and denial. Day in day out, real men and women who are in retirement right now are enjoying all the cream of the proverbial ice in that they enjoy everything while others sit back and think about how life is unfair, unfulfilling or how everyone has abandoned them.

While it is true that life isn't always fair and that sometimes, even the best of us can be dealt a bad hand, this book stands to serve as a practical guide towards actively confronting many of the difficult and challenging issues that retirees face. It is not a denial that challenges exist; rather, it is an affirmation of them.

My goal is writing this book is to demonstrate that there is a path towards personal satisfaction and happiness in retirement. Its goal is to ensure that we are maximizing the enormous value of time that we have been allotted in this special period in our lives. It wasn't so long ago in fact, that for many people, living past 50 or even 40 years of age was considered "ancient" and strange!

Getting everything said and done is one of the craziest things that people really don't know and quite frankly, frequently don't have a clue about. So very often, the first step, the step of realizing that we need a plan moving ahead, is very often the hardest step and certainly the most critical.

For many people who would love to be that so-called ideal man or woman in retirement; they would want to have everything attractively laid out in front of them all the way from the look to the touch of class. However, without the right plan or the right attitude, one can easily fall victim to the numerous potholes along with the path towards personal fulfilment. Retirement is not simply a matter of feeling good; but also an existential question that will, in the final analysis, impact the people around you including the people whom you love and cherish.

This book makes the case that retirement, far from being the end of anything is actually the start of a new passage in life. It is, for most people, an entirely different journey and way of looking at the world and at the relationships around us than before. From matters concerning loved ones to finances to spiritual well-being, much of what we have become familiar with and accustomed to has now changed irreversibly.

It is how we deal with that change – both in ourselves in the world around that we reach our goals and aspirations.

Introduction

Have you retired or are planning to retire anytime soon? Does retirement reality check scare you a little bit or even result in a cold sweat? Have you ever thought of planning on your retirement plans fully? Have you considered the numbers of years and decades that you will remain in retirement? What about money and finances? How will you continue to remain active – socially, physically, and spiritually – during your retirement years?

These and many additional questions are some of the things this book will fully explore and provide answers for so that we are holistically prepared on this all-important period in our lives.

There are so many things that people take for granted in the sense that, they always assume that everything will be up and running without thinking twice. Wise moves in your retirement decision-making will be tackled to ensure that individuals are fully focused and aware of how each and every move they make not only affects their future but also impacts their loved ones as well.

The main principle and intention of this book is to understand these issues and concerns with regards to retirement and come up with a unique solution. The best solution of course is always linked to a better working plan beyond any reasonable doubt that is focused on ensuring quality information that is served to the letter.

First and foremost, just to get this out of the way, retirement is not a death sentence not does it signify that your life is "over". It is just a sign that you are growing older and other generations are catching up with you. A new phase in your life is beginning or perhaps has already begun in earnest. This guide will ensure that you are set and focused through the various aspects of life in retirement. Relevant and pertinent information and material will be given so that you have the power to make sound and intelligent decisions concerning your future. But first, it is vitally important that we ask the right questions that will form the foundation of this journey together to ensure that your unique retirement plan is executed and that you understand its consequences completely.

1. **Proper definition of retirement**

    What is retirement exactly and why does it scare so many people? Get an inside deal on the best definition of retirement. Discover the timeline of retirement age and different organizations that offer benefits to retirees.

2. **Is retirement focused on age only?**

   Learn all the facts about retirement packages and understand the true repercussions and ripple effects that retirement has on your life through various levels.

3. **Is there an exact amount of money I should retire with?**

   Understand better if there is a proper way to retire and ensure that everything is going as planned according to your own unique goals and vision about what you want in life.

   This book will discuss how and why you should build a "nest

egg" or emergency fund for unforeseen calamities and accidents even for those who are extremely confident about their ability to work hard and save.

The sad and tragic issues concerning loss of loved ones and close family members and how to properly go through the grieving process will also be explored.

4. **Pros and cons of competing retirement plans and visions**

Learn all the pros and cons plus factors that determine the best package to choose from based on retirement plans. Understanding how to balance your savings with quality of life concerns; re-connecting with family, maintaining an active and healthy lifestyle and incorporating technology into your regimen will all be fully discussed and examined.

All the pros and cons will be fully explained to ensure that every step that is taken is always truly a step in the right direction towards holistic fulfilment.

OVERVIEW OF WHAT RETIREMENT TRULY MEANS

Retirement as a matter of fact, is being in a position to leave your daily work routine fully due to age factors mostly. There are other factors that might lead to retirement also and are typically referred as early retirement. Retirement is not about quitting or getting fired at all. Quitting and getting fired is a termination of employment made because it is agree upon either mutually or typically by one party that the working relationship is no longer a good fit for business or institution.

To ensure that everything goes as planned in all retirement packages, there are serious planning steps that need to be covered beyond reasonable doubt. As they say, failing to plan is always planning to fail. Retirement plans should be taken cautiously to ensure that retired individuals get a better package and benefits.

The right age to retire always differs with employers, businesses, government or public sector jobs, job description and design plus any age restrictions. In most cases, 65 years is the average age of retirement. This will ensure that everything is covered and sorted fully for the individuals to enjoy the rest of their lives. There are so many things that always come in line with retirement in the sense that, you will only get a better deal if everything is fully planned.

As a matter of fact, so many people fail to plan on their retirement package and as a result, they end up running up and down when the date is due. One way or the other, to ensure that every deal goes as planned, there are so many things that we should never take for granted at all. The critical part of ensuring that you are safe from retirement stroke is that, 10 to 15 years of your final lap should always be independent from the numerations attached to the organization.

Whether true or false, there are so many things that we should never take for granted at all. When it comes to ensuring that everything is running as planned, better planning strategies should always be applied to avoid disaster. As they always say, prevention is always the best remedy in one way or the other. To be on the safe side of retirement shock, early preparation should be put in place.

This book is here to help you understand further what retirement truly means. Why we have to retire and how we should retire. It will give you an inside story with detailed information on how best we can maneuver around retirement plans, what to do to avoid retirement disappointment and the basic requirements needed to ensure that you are safe from retirement shock.

This book will fully enlighten those who are at the verge of joining the ranks of those who are already retired as well as those that have already taken the plunge in one form or another and are now looking for advice to how to re-organize their lives and try to make some sense of what can be a challenging period of transition.

Topic 1: The Journey Beings

Adjusting to retirement physically, mentally and spiritually

There are so many things that we should never take for granted when it comes to ensuring that retirement doesn't surprise you at all. So many people really don't care about planning just because they say they say they are not really planning to live forever and express certainty of enjoying full service of what they planned for is uncertain. Holding other factors constant, there are a few things that we should never take for granted beyond when it comes to ensuring that we are enjoying full retirement benefits.

There are so many things that should be ensured it has been covered beyond reasonable doubt to be able to fully enjoy full retirement package that always comes our way one way or the other. The transition period from work to retirement is what so many people really don't know how to tackle fully. There are various stages that will ensure that you are enjoying fully all the retirement steps to ensure that it doesn't catch you an aware.

Planning for your retirement as early as possible is key. It is in fact one of things that should never be taken for granted at all. If retirement catches you unaware, an adjustment period that should be followed is totally different to a person who had planned and ensured that they are in fact fully prepared.

As much as some of the things that we always take for granted have bigger and better meaning, there are always serious consequences that always follow when you don't plan as early as possible. Sensible and careful planning will undoubtedly save you time and heartache in the future.

As a matter of fact, some of the retirement techniques that should be followed to the letter should include the fact that mental, physical and psychological adjustment should be handled carefully.

Mental adjustment

When it comes to ensuring that everything is set, here are some of the things that should never be taken for granted at all. As matter of fact, one thing that should never be taken for granted is the fact that, retirement is a must process that we will always face. It is a phase of our life that we will only enjoy based on the fact that, things should be planned as early as 10 to 15 years prior to retirement age.

To be safe mentally and ensure that you don't really suffer mentally, you will have to accept the reality check that you are indeed on a new path in life. Accepting the fact that retirement is real is the only way we will be in a position to enjoy fully all the benefits of retirement. In order to reach these material benefits, you should try as much as possible to ensure that you are living a positive and constructive life; one that, as much as possible is free from the stress, hecticness and constant worry that has become all too common in our daily lives.

Regretting that you are fired, retrenched or that you are in a medical condition that doesn't allow you to work anymore is something that we should take positively and try to make the best of it. There are so many things that we can do to ensure that we are retirement proof in terms of surprises. Some of the surprises are never that serious while others are of course very serious.

Enjoying each and every minute that you are given because you are now retired is something that we should all focus on since it is the best food for the soul and mind. Enjoying oneself should be handled responsibly to avoid squandering all the bonuses and golden handshakes that come with it.

Physical adjustment

Retirement based on age might come as a shock to those who don't really plan at all. Planning is the only factor that will ensure that, everything goes as you wish one way or the other. There are serious consequences that always come when we literally ignore future planning. To be able to enjoy all the benefits that might come when you retire, early retirement planning should be part of your plans as early as possible.

There are so many things that people take for granted and assume that they will never fall victim to at all until the day they are faced with that cold reality check. Not everybody will always plan to get sick or get into an accident or inquire if the company's plan to get dissolved at all. It all comes incidentally and some people suffer as victims.

You will only be able to enjoy this time fully when it comes to retirement if you have planned fully on what you should do when something happens to your current occupation. Physical adjustment is a factor that should never be taken for granted at all. So many people decide that, due to the disappointment they are facing, they will just sit and watch TV all day, become coach potatoes, or sleep and just relax all day every day.

Relaxing and doing nothing at all just because you think you have nothing to do is not the best idea at all. In fact, it is ultimately destructive as it takes away from your energy and passion. So many people who take retirement as a plan to kill them softly are the ones who should try as much as they possibly can to enroll themselves into positive living and enjoy retirement fully. There are quite a number of retirement packages that we should never take for granted at all. The best solution should be based on the fact that we should always be physically fit to enjoy the fruits of retirement.

Going for nature walks, morning and evening runs plus signing in for gym classes should always be incorporated into a healthy lifestyle plan one way or the other. Some people enroll in playing their favorite sport so that they remain active and also afford themselves the opportunity to socialize with others. Being and staying physically active ensures you are leading a healthy lifestyle and doing so with others helps to avoid the psychological torture of total isolation.

Spiritual Adjustment

Part of the adjustment procedure that retired people should always undergo is, to get the best training and preparation on matters concerning spiritual adjustment. This is often an overlooked and even neglected aspect in this time period. Spiritual adjustment is focused on the fact that, you should have the morale that you had before retirement; it means feeding and nurturing the soul so that no matter what type of journey you inevitably face, you will be content and confident going forward.

Some people hunker down and fail to handle anything that comes their way with the kind of positive energy that they had just because they retired. Approaching retirement from a perspective of positive vibes and feelings is a powerful factor when it comes to being spiritually fulfilled. As a matter of fact, there are so many things that we can do to ensure so that we are enjoying our lives in retirement better than ever before. Facing the bull and taking it down by the horns is always the best idea but, playing wise moves should be part of everyone's plan.

There are many things that will ensure spiritual adjustment is taken positively by the decisions that we make. Based on the fact that, retirement is not a "death sentence", we can turn it into achievable goals and desires fully.

Think of it this way: consider all the projects, hobbies, ideas you had but were just too busy when you were working and/or taking care of your family to fully devote yourself to. Now you no longer have the excuse – you now have that time to embark on whatever project your heart should elect to pursue. The question is only one of desire and motivation.

To ensure that the challenges are faced and you emerge victorious, there is a spiritual factor that should never be taken for granted at all.

Some of the spiritual adjustment issues that can be sorted should include the fact that, you should live a positive life. Try as much as possible to ensure that everything is sorted beyond a reasonable doubt to be on the safe side. Turning all the lemons that life might throw at you into lemonade should always be your priority and strategy to success.

I am by no means advocating a turn to religion if that is not you; for some people a greater sense of spirituality simply means attending a church, synagogue, temple or mosque and forging an ever-closer relationship with other parishioners while for others attaining a higher spirituality means forging a closer relationship with nature and for others it means exploring a personal, private relationship with God.

Whatever path you choose and whatever is your road towards spiritual renewal and vitality that is right for you is the one that makes you wake up and get out of bed with a smile while motivated to pursue your day with confidence and buoyancy.

CHAPTER TWO MANAGING MONEY

Business tricks for retired people
Secrets for Getting Your Business Loan Approved

Money is one of the biggest concerns facing retirees and no for no small reason. The idea of only living off social security or a pension is a frightening prospect for many. This section explores the many opportunities that are available for retirees to make money, save money and have the realization that, far from being an end, retirement can actually be the start of an entirely and potentially lucrative part of your life.

For many small businessmen, the first step is securing capital through a business loan. In order for your loan to be approved in the fastest manner an entrepreneur whether a first timer or an experienced entrepreneur that wants to boost his business one has to be on the top notch of his or her game to increase the chances of getting it approved without so much ado. The following are some of the ways to get your loan approved.

Forging a good relationship with your local bank: One is required to build a good relationship with the bank, prior to borrowing a loan from them or any other lending firms. Ensure that you have a credible account with them and make it active be it a personal account or a business account. Make sure there is enough cash flow in terms of depositing cash into the account with no zero balances, bounced checks to avoid punitive fees and penalties. Make sure the rapport created with your bank is long lasting to earn you marks of getting your loan application approved as fast as possible when you will need the loan.

Many seniors and retirees have noted how their local banks not only offer better terms but also superior treatment as valued customers rather than just a number. The Utah Community Bank, for instance, offers a $100 Amazon gift card for opening a home equity loan and a free Apple watch for opening a mortgage with them! While obviously no important financial decision should be made on promotions alone, it does demonstrate a greater desire to earn your business than say, many a giant retail bank whose *only modus operandi* seems to be to fleece you as much as possible! Check out community banks and credit better in your area for the latest offerings and deals.

Business Plan: If you are seriously considering starting your own business or entrepreneurial endeavor, bear in mind that the bank will inquire about the kind of business you want to venture in. share your business plan with them so as for them to clearly see that you are well aware of what you have at hand and how you plan to operate the business to maximize on the returns. The business plan should have approximately three to five years of realistic financial projections so as to show the bank that you are a serious long term business and the possibility of growth is there and ultimately, the ability to repay your loan is there.

Financial advice: make sure that you get an honest or rather an experienced banker to advise you accordingly sine he/she will reveal to you what the bank expects from you before trusting their money with you. They will outlay all the criteria used by the bank to get potential borrowers.

Entrepreneurial skills for retired people

Being an entrepreneur is something that most people dream of. Being self employed, having team members that can be trusted and seeing the business grow is what attracts them to entrepreneurship. There are difficult situations that will be experienced no matter how well the business runs. . Having the spirit of an entrepreneur is what keeps people going. Facing challenges that come up will help you do better in every challenge or difficult situation that arises in the future. Entrepreneurship and business includes taking action and being in control of your own destiny. The first thing about being a successful entrepreneur is coming up with an idea. You should have an idea in a field that you have experience or interest in. You should also be willing to learn more on the industry and market to give you an upper hand. This makes it easier to plan and strategize on attaining and maintaining clients.

Successful entrepreneurs should always have a strong passion and persistent desire to maintain and or improve the business state. Do what is necessary to eliminate negative talk by chanting, praying and taking necessary the necessary course of action; in others do what you feel needs to be done in order to attain and maintain a thoroughly positive attitude.

As an entrepreneur you should always think about yourself as the strong, capable and compassionate person you are.

Discounts and Budgets

One of the great perks about joining the ranks of retired individuals is the amount of great discounts that are readily available to you. Very often, everything from local restaurants, diners, to local consignment stores will have special discounts for seniors. Joining an organization like the AARP will further give you opportunities to save money and get valuable discounts on everything from travel-related expenses, hotels, clothing, entertainment and even grocery shopping.

Maintaining a budget and understanding the limitations of your income and adjusting your spending habits accordingly is another key towards achieving a pleasant and stress-free retirement. One powerful way to do so is by creating a Retirement Calculator whereby you simply add up all of your sources of income and deduct it from all of your expenses. But be careful! It is always best to take a conservative approach to doing so and allotting a certain amount of expenses for unforeseen events e.g. accidents, injuries, and serious medical issues.

Creating a budget is perhaps a relatively easy endeavor and one in which you probably have a great deal of experience in. The difficulty and the challenge lies in having the discipline to stick to it and do so in a manner that allows for unfortunate, unforeseen situations that we don't always prepare for.

Let me use a personal example. I became acquainted with a retired gentleman named Pete from Richmond, Virginia. He was always a big saver; he didn't need any lectures on saving money he informed me, he's been doing so his entire life! A fair point I thought to myself, after all, this is a man with a lifetime of budgeting and he further told me that he prided himself on living within his means.

Unfortunately for Pete, he suffered a series of catastrophic accidents that took him completely by surprise. First, while driving to the store, Pete had to swerve his car at a severe angle to avoid hitting a deer but by doing so lost control of his car and hit a tree in a head-on collision. This results in a total loss of his motor vehicle. What made matters worse for him was that as a result of the accident, his nagging back problems worsened to the point where expensive surgery was now required. His wife Susan also had a car accident with this time period and although fortunately she was free from physical harm, the car repair bill was in the thousands.

Tragically, all this happened within a fortnight. In other words, it did not happen in a progressive or elongated manner in which one could pay off for each dilemma piecemeal; it happened almost all at once. In a matter of days, Pete's savings had been wiped out completely.

I do not relay this story to scare anyone; certainly, even non-retirees can have unlucky events impact them in profound ways. The point however, is that retirees often don't have the same means to recover from severe financial loss. It makes sense to maintain a conservative attitude with your finances and have an "emergency" fund for those types of unforeseen situations.

While no one can ever prepare fully for the emotional, physical and financial trauma of heartbreaking accident, one can begin the process of creating a fund to mitigate the effects so it is at least less depilating to your financial well-being.

Always remember to regularly consult with your financial planner. Do not make the mistake that many make and ignore bad or troublesome financial developments in the hope that it will simply disappear on its own. Now is the time to take a pro-active role when it comes to your personal finances and investments. Remember, no one cares more about your money than you do.

No one is more affected by the financial decisions that you make than you are. Keep this in mind, regularly consult and stay on top of any retirement accounts, IRAs or investment portfolios that you own and demand accountability from those whom are entrusted with your hard-earned cash.

Downsizing – The Case for an Affordable Transition in Retirement

It may seem counterintuitive at first. You might say, "Downsize?!? Why? My kids have left the nest egg (finally!), my house is paid for and I no longer have to deal with the expenses of commuting to work, why should I not live large and reap the rewards of decades of all my hard work?"

While such an attitude may be tempting, it's actually time to consider doing the opposite. Roger was one of my closest friends and also one of the hardest-working men that I know. He worked incredibly hard and was devoted to his family. He also believed that he would never retire; he was "old school" of a different generation and told me often that he would be happiest if he passed away while working on the job.

While such a view may be admirable in certain respects, sadly, Roger always planned his finances as if he would continue working non-stop and continue making progressively larger and larger amounts of money. He maintained a large house, opened up a second mortgage to pay for an bigger expansion of his property and purchased two brand new vehicles through separate car loans taking advantage of his excellent credit. Roger loved to work hard and play hard as many hard working people are apt to do. When Roger was physically no longer able to work, he did not take it well. At first, he remained in denial until family was forced to take care of him and he would remain under their care for the rest of his life. Unfortunately, during this time period, the bills didn't stop coming. The mortgage, the loans, the bills kept on coming unrelentingly. Roger kept on investing more and more into a house that contained fewer and fewer people as his wife passed away and kids moved out years ago.

He refused to live within his means, or perhaps more accurately, refused to adjust his lifestyle as he was rapidly entering into a new period in his life. Life doesn't stop because we refuse to accept its consequences; it remains unrelenting despite our wishes.

That is why it is important to downsize. It is a recognition that we may not need the huge house we owned before when we had a big family and were responsible for several children. It may mean transitioning to a condo or an apartment instead of a large home; it can also mean staying with family for a period of time. Hard-working personalities can consider launching a business from home to stay active or working on a part-time or voluntary basis at one of the many worthwhile charity organizations out there.

For other retirees who live in high-tax and high cost of living states, it may mean moving to a more senior friendly and economically affordable environment. In the US, there are many states that are favorable for retirees and senior citizens. Florida is famous for its large senior citizen population and its warm weather, cheap real estate when compared with other states, and no state income tax. Other relatively low-cost of living states to consider for retirees who are no longer interested in brutal winters would be Texas, Kansas, Nevada, Arizona and Kentucky.

Some rather adventurous retirees even take an international route and incorporate their love of travel into their decisis ion and consider enclaves such as Costa Rica for their retirement home while others do not wish to be that far apart from family.

Never compare yourself and your success with others. Your success depends on this fact. Believe in your uniqueness and you will prevail.

Always remember that your financial goals and your retirement goals are personal to you alone! The needs, spending habits, lifestyle choices and so on varies greatly depending on the resolutions that we make as individuals. Don't let someone else's retirement goals have any influence or bearing over your own!

TOPIC THREE – FAMILY LIFE

How to remain active in your family's life even though they may seem too busy to spend time with you

Retirement can be lonely to many of us. You have spent your entire life on your career and you may not have dedicated enough time to your family. Once you have retired, you realize that you now have all the time in the world but your children and grandchildren may not have any time for you! It may be hard to transition from a previously active schedule into a relaxed lifestyle that is committed to the development of your family.

During such times, it is good to look back and reflect. As you move into yet another phase of your life, deepening the connection that you have with family is paramount. You can adopt the following ways to enhance relations with your family.

Take Part in Sporting Activities Together

Sports help bond you together as a family. You can organize for such family excursions such as hikes or various sporting events and involve your family. This will help you maintain close relationships with them and even bring you closer as you remain in your active family life. Private or community swimming pools are a great, fun way to either exercise or relax as it allows for a wide array of activities from very different levels of intensity.

You as Teacher – Why every retiree should be a teacher at some point

You may not think of yourself as a teacher but the fact of the matter is your life experiences alone are enough to put many instructors to shame! It is important that you share your knowledge and what you have learned from throughout your life with others.

Alternatively, you may consider enrolling in a community college that offers affordable tuition and may even offer supplemental benefits for seniors. A great example is the Northern Virginia Community College that offers (wait for it) free tuition for seniors that are 60 years or older and lived in Virginia for at least one year. You should inquire in your town whether similar programs exist. Think of the opportunity of learning with a professor and classmates about literature, that language you always wanted to learn but never had the time or exploring a fascinating historical time period that you always wanted to learn more about.

As you are learning yourself, what a great way to turnkey that information and explain what you are learning about with your family! It makes you sound dynamic and interesting to younger family members – "Guess who's going back to school kids!" Or maybe you can even pose a friendly challenge asking them to compare grades!

On a serious note however, imparting knowledge on younger generations is an important way for many seniors to stay relevant and open up the lines of communication with family members. Don't cut yourself short – regardless of your level of education, you have a lot of important lessons to share even on a "common sense" level. You might be surprised at some of the things that you may believe everyone knows (writing a check or even writing in cursive for instance) that many have no clue about! So don't keep all that knowledge to yourself, share it with family and friends!

Take part in ensuring that they grow in their spiritual life

You can take a lead role in ensuring that your family members grow in their spirituality. If you are religious, accompany them to the temple, mosque or church. Be actively involved in guiding them with their various engagements. Perhaps most importantly, offer your sound advice and wisdom to your family and especially to your grandchildren. Many are in need of spiritual guidance even if they don't often ask for it or show it. Being a spiritual leader in your family will give you a renewed purpose in life and also make you feel that you are making powerful contributions to the transcendent needs of your loved ones.

Take a much deeper interest in your children or grandchildren's hobbies

Even if you no longer live with your children or grandchildren you can take a deeper interest in their hobbies. This may be sports or academic interests that seem to grab their attention. By doing this, you get to form much closer bonds with them. You can accompany them to sporting events or in contests that they actively participate in. Cheering them up and motivating them serves as a big boost in showing that you care for them and are truly committed to their growth. When you can, teach them new skills or hobbies that would make them more useful members in society. This way, they would always be grateful to you and proactively inquire whether grandpa or grandpa will be attending their sporting event, performance, play, or contest!

Surprise them once in a while

You can organize to surprise relatives once in a while. Do so in simple ways such as making breakfast for them and leaving them notes just to show how much you care for them. Or you can organize a retreat for your family on one of the holidays so you get together and enjoy yourselves.

When you are actively involved in all of these things, you will slowly realize that you have a lead role in the affairs of your family. You will be their go to guy/lady when they have issues that they are dealing with. You will also see that whenever they are free, they would love to spend more time with you. You can always be on the lookout for more innovative ways to spend time with them. A good example would be watching the latest movies or music videos with them from their favorite actor or musician whenever you can. While watching one of their programs may not be your, er, "cup of tea" the point of course is to create bonds with them, open up the lines of communication, and show interest in their lives as well. Young people often get a rise out of watching an older person from a different generation respond to one of their favorite "cutting edge" artists. Little do they know you have very likely seen it all before! You may offer up a surprise or two for them when they realize that grandpa or grandma isn't so "naive" about the world as they may have been led to believe! Use this to your advantage! This will definitely endear you especially to the younger generation.

How to make your visits mutually beneficial so that you also feel that you are a contributing member of your family

There are so many things that people take for granted in the sense that people will always be around to build and share memories with. Living a better life will only make sense after retiring when you are busy visiting those you didn't visit before. To ensure that everything goes as planned, you should never think of yourself as a bother at all when you visit with a reason.

Visiting family and friends with a purpose ensures that everything goes as planned. Planning to live a better life after retirement should be a way to enjoy your newfound freedom. Visiting friends should be something that is done on a daily basis; however, for some if you overdo the visitation then it may become a problem.

There are so many things that we always think is appropriate yet, it ends up confusing us. Taking other people's time for granted is not good at all because, you will always be depicted as the bad guy one way or the other. These are serious things that should never be taken for granted at all when it comes to matters of feelings. Different people will have different definitions of fun and they might not be willing to enjoy with you.

To ensure that everything goes as planned, you will only be satisfied when you don't take everything for granted at all. Some of the things that we should verify before going to any family meeting should be:

1. Ensuring that everyone is free
2. Free time is enjoyed and is mutually beneficial
3. Purpose of visitation has been defined
4. Duration has been established
5. Parameters have been agreed upon or established beforehand

How to explore your community for events and activities that are senior-friendly to make new

friends or spend time with old ones

Ask retirees who are enjoying their time fully and they will be the first ones to tell you that participating in a variety of activities is a great way to have fun and feel youthful. There are so many things that retired people will find entertaining, when they meet and try to work together.

The best part of it is the fact that, we will always enjoy them responsibly if we have the right people around us.

A key part of ensuring that you are enjoying and mingling with the right people should be:

1. Throwing a party that fits your age bracket should always be

our first priority. This will give you the right people you would love to have and relate to in a friendly fashion.

2. Walk down memory lane: Taking a walk down memory lane will give you a throwback feeling and brings together those who were there that time. Examples include: that diner where you met your sweetheart or that local restaurant where you met with friends or going back to that park where you used to have walks either by yourself or with your significant other.

3. The theme should be 20-30 years ago: having it that way ensures that you will give said event the appropriate definition and theme which will be understood by the attendees.

4. Old School Theme: Having an old school theme will never disappoint at all! You will always enjoy it fully when it comes to these types of themes because it will bring back powerful memories within that time period and encourage your friends – both close and perhaps those that have been "forgotten" – a chance to come back and re-enter your social

circle. This will give you confidence about being the organizer of the event and also allow you to enjoy the company of folks within that age bracket.

Topic 4: Dealing with Loss

Everyone must ultimately encounter loss of loved ones at some point. Unfortunately at this age, many people experience it more often than they did previously. Many seniors react differently and take the impact differently based on the fact that they might have been hit by a bigger and even worse circumstance that the current situation.

There are so many things that will always happen at the age of 60 plus years. This is the age that most people will feel they have achieved what they wanted in life or perhaps are under the false assumption that they can achieve no more – such notions would be easily dispelled by reading the biography of one Cornelius Vanderbilt. Vanderbilt, well-known for being the great tycoon of the railroad business, only began buying up the independent railroads when he was approaching 70 years of age! Clearly, he did not believe that his life was over, far from it! And it's also worth considering that he did so in the middle of the 19th century with life expectancy rates far lower than what they are today.

For other seniors, their ambitions are far more down to earth. Truly, the only things they want are to sit back and watch their kids and grand children grow older and older as they share memories and unforgettable moments with them.

As much as death is something that nobody would love to associate with beyond any reasonable doubt, it is a reality check and also it bears keeping in mind that we will always be comfortable when we think we have everything planned. It is never the best part or time of our lives at all when we have been hit by such a tragedy. It literally confirms that no one is here forever one way or the other and that we are all in fact very mortal. It is not something any normal person can look forward to, but it is something that one can learn to take a philosophical perspective on by focusing on what they did during their life and the good deeds they left behind as memories to be cherished forever.

Being retired confirms that you have done your nation proud serving them for the time you have been productive to date.

Loss and death is something that we should accept just like the way we accepted retirement and learn to slowly, gradually accept. It is the only road that we will all pass through eventually.

How to cope with loss of loved ones, especially the traumatic loss of a spouse
How to cope with the loss of family members and loved ones, especially the traumatic loss of a spouse is not

simple at all. Often, the most painful and heartbreaking losses comes when you hear about a couple that has been married for 30, 40 or even 50 years only to hear that someone's wife or husband passed away. It is difficult for even the greatest of communicators to know exactly what to say in these kinds of situations.

From the outside, all you can do is be there to support that person who is grieving and offer them your unequivocal support. Just like in retirement, it takes time to ensure that you have fully recovered from such a sad event. There is nothing wrong and in fact it is actually quite essential to give yourself room and space to deal with this painful loss.

It is very important to allow for yourself or for loved ones a grieving period to honor the dead and those that have recently passed away.

This grieving process is totally normal and healthy. The most important aspect in this is really talking to people about what just happened and sharing memories of that person together. Remember that trying to live a positive life is one of the best things that we should always try to do. As they say, time is always one of the best of the best healers. You will always recover fully from your loss as time goes by; honor those that are no longer with us, and continue to be engaged with your family and friends.

Do not abandon your intimate social circle; for they are needed now more than ever.

It might not be an easy step but all in all, accepting and moving on is the difficult answer to many problems that we will eventually have to face.

Maintaining a social network for support

Talking to relatives, family and friends always comes in handy in the sense that, you will always get better. Keeping all of your problems, worries and concerns to yourself is one of the sure-fire ways that we can start to feel isolated and eventually depressed. Dealing with your problems alone might seem like a good decision but you will face all of your problems alone and without the social support and feedback that all humans need.

Having people around you who are focused on ensuring that everything goes as planned is one of the many things that we should never take for granted. As a matter of fact, you will only be safe and ready to confront all of your problems when you are talking to people.

Talking and being open to people will give you that power and chance to do something meaningful. The only surething we have should be based on the fact that we are talking to people that love us, care about us, and are concerned about our well-being.

No matter what, you will only get a better solution when you decide to talk to people who will always add value to your life and happiness and personal fulfillment.

Adding value will only play a critical role if we are open to receiving it. The best advice in the world will be entirely useless if it falls on deaf ears; so let us be open to our family and friends during trying times, even if it sometimes goes against our intuition.

For they are the lifeboats we will need to get through the stormy seas of loss and inner turmoil.

Topic Five: Being Tech Savvy

How seniors and retirees can navigate through an unfamiliar world of gadgets and high-tech devices

Technology is something that, fortunately or unfortunately, will continue to remain a huge part of the modern world. The only opportunity we get as a matter of fact, will only be manifested fully when we know what we really want out of it. Technology is something that will keep changing day by day to meet different customer demands. It is truly incredible to witness the almost surreal manner in which cutting-edge technology becomes obsolete in a matter of months if not sooner!

Many seniors note that the younger generation appears to spend more time behind screens and mobile devices than they do in the real world – very often, they are correct in this regard!

All of this makes for a strange world that can seem rather intimidating to many seniors. While most will never reach the level of technological proficiency that our grandchildren currently enjoy, we can strive to achieve a comfort level so that technology enters into a cautious alliance with us rather than an adversarial relationship.

Some people might just be stuck in the only system that worked several years or decades back when they used to be youths or in their teens. To ensure that everything goes smoothly in terms of technology, you will only advance if you know what you want.

Following tech sites that provide specific, easy to understand instructions about technologies without all of the confusing jargon will ensure that you are up to date in terms of gadgets and tech devices. Some people decide to follow technology news sites that give you relevant updates that keep popping up day by day. There are many things that we can be certain about when it comes to technology in the sense that clients will never be disappointed when it comes to their satisfaction. The amount of pleasure and satisfaction derived from using a modern device is more awe-inspiring compared with using traditional or old-school gadgets that are rapidly becoming obsolete.

It always starts with an individual then it develops to something bigger and better. If you accept to have technology – whether it be a laptop, Kindle, Ipad, smartphone, tablet and so on- be a substantial part of your life you will be able to pick and choose when and where technology can work for you and complement your life.

As a matter of fact, there are serious gadgets and devices that keep coming and getting updated every day which are specifically geared towards making the lives of seniors and retirees better.

One such example is the PERS or Personal Emergency Response system. Polls indicated that, unsurprisingly, the vast majority of seniors wish to remain in their homes rather than in care centers. With the PERS technology this is now much more feasible. The PERS device allows for seniors to call for help with just the push of a button. It gives them and their families peace of mind that help is only a push away.

Another example is a device many may be already familiar with. Skype and other online services allow for retirees to remain in contact with loved ones virtually when meeting them physically is no longer possible. Finally, video game and virtual reality systems may not be just for kids! As a matter of fact, retirees may find them to be incredibly useful as low-intensity exercise programs that can help them to remain physically fit and active within the confines of their own home. This is an important way that we can not only have fun, but maintain good health that will lead to a longer and more fulfilling quality of life as we age and continue to mature.

So tell your grandson to stop playing that car racing or fighting video game; grandpa and grandma now need some time on that system as well!

Free or cheap ways seniors can improve their tech proficiency

The easiest way a senior citizen can improve on technology is going through the updates that come by. There are so many ways you will be able to ensure that you are fully updated bar that, you are focused on improving your adeptness with regards to technology.

With all the news sites, email updates and booklets on tech tools and gadgets, there is no way you will be in a position to settle for a product that is not worth your money. Technology will be improving on a daily basis to ensure that it meets customer demands and specifications. Meeting all the design, descriptions and expectations should always be a priority.

Another way of familiarizing oneself with technology is simply by taking a bold, "hands on" approach with them. Simply by "playing" or toying with such devices will make you more comfortable with it than perhaps spending an inordinate amount of time fretting over its precise usage.

Having the right product and one in which you are willing to consume all of its contents to the letter is another way of making sure that everything goes as planned. Planning to advance is a step that we all have in mind but putting the plans to practice is the main goal towards completing our agenda of achieving a comfortable level of technological proficiency and awareness.

Remember that while we may never be as tech-friendly as our grandkids, it doesn't mean we have to be scared of these gadgets either – by selectively incorporating technology when it is to our benefit and to our advantage is the best way of maximizing their value to our busy lives!

Conclusion

The only remedy you will ever gain at the end of any transaction is having the best of the best solution of a problem made available to you. In short, information is power; knowledge is power.

Many people are struggling to find their own niche in retirement. They feel isolated and even worthless. The goal here is to begin to formulate that plan along with our goals for self-fulfilment. There are so many people who would love to become Alpha men (or women!) since they are deemed as cool and desirable. But they often forget the real deal behind a successful

Alpha man and woman when it comes to retirement.

Conversely, many people think that retirement is a walk in the park until they try and realise that they were totally wrong. There are many things that you have to accomplish in order to be fully satisfied mentally, spiritually, physically and emotionally.

If there is one last last thing I would like to instill it is that by incorporating a holistic approach that addresses all of your unique needs as an individual will ultimately be the best way towards creating a happy and successful retirement.

A complete program will always be useful when everything is put into practice rather than remain idle in someone's notebook. Successful transformation of an amateur to a professional ready, willing and able to handle all of the challenges of retirement with confidence is the goal.

Retirement is the start of something new; it is a new chapter in your life that you must accept with open arms.

It is important that we do not enter this new epoch with naiveté or with dispassion; but accept it as another step on the path towards a complete existence; another road on the journey we call life.

Whether your goal is to imitate or even transcend the financial success of someone like Vanderbilt; achieve lasting spiritual fulfilment; or to simply remain content and excited by being an active part and playing a leadership role within your family, the final goals and parameters of what makes a successful retirement is yours and yours alone. I hope this guide has helped you arrive closer to creating for you that vision and lastly, the realization that life has in fact, only just begun.

Retirement Book Camp Checklist

- ✓ Budget, save and always leave a significant amount for unforeseen events

- ✓ Seek spiritual enrichment to help you reach and maintain a high level of motivation

- ✓ Become a leader and "go to" person within your family

- ✓ Think of retirement as being the start of a new journey in life rather than the end of anything

- *Explore and take advantage of local discounts and consider joining organizations that promote the goal of supporting seniors financially*

- *Loss is something we all have to sadly deal with. Use your family and social networks as pillars of support in these difficult times*

- *Routinely review your finances with your financial adviser or planner*

- *It is almost always far better to confront an issue or challenge rather than pretend it doesn't exist or that it will go away on its own*

- ✓ *Make time for yourself - this is the perfect opportunity to take on that new project you always wanted to start but never had the time to do so. Start that project and that new hobby without hesitation or excuses. This is your time!*

- ✓ *Maintain your physical well—being and a healthy lifestyle. Take long walks and invite friends to join you.*

- *Reminisce. Sometimes it is important to go "back in time" and revisit some of the places that we enjoyed back in our youth. Relive happy memoires of the past and think about how you will make new ones!*

- *Tame Technology. Technology can be intimidating but we should learn how to use them when they make our lives easier and help us re-connect with loved ones*

- *Create a retirement plan right now and include your goals in it*

- ✓ *Whenever you feel that you are becoming depressed or despondent, open yourself up to others- family, friends, church parishioners, club members and so on. By opening ourselves up we begin to understand the influence and social impact we have on our families and communities*

- ✓ *Understand that there is no one uniform plan for everyone. Why? Because we all have our own goals and lifestyles; we have very different ideas of what a successful retirement is:*

for some this means maximizing income, for others it means spending as much time with family as possible and for others it might simply be relaxing and taking that vacation you always to take but never found the time

- ✓ *Learning to be at peace with yourself and achieving fulfilment on a holistic level will give you lasting and meaningful happiness as you embark on this new and fascinating time period in your life*

List of My Retirement Goals

_____

_____

_____

_____

_____

_____

_____

_____

_____

_____

_____

_____

_____

www.ingramcontent.com/pod-product-compliance
Lightning Source LLC
Chambersburg PA
CBHW030848180526
45163CB00004B/1496